Everyone Prays: Celebrating Faith Around the World
© 2014 Text Alexis York Lumbard,
Artwork World Wisdom, Inc.

Wisdom Tales is an imprint of World Wisdom, Inc.

Library of Congress Cataloging-in-Publication Data

Lumbard, Alexis York, 1981-
  Everyone prays : celebrating faith around the world / by Alexis York
Lumbard ; illustrated by Alireza Sadeghian.
    pages cm
  ISBN 978-1-937786-19-9 (hardcover : alk. paper) 1. Prayer--Juvenile
literature. 2. Religions--Juvenile literature. I. Sadeghian, Alireza, 1980-
illustrator. II. Title.
  BL560.L86 2014
  204'.3--dc23

2013037644

Printed in China on acid-free paper
Production Date: October 2013; Plant & Location: Printed by Everbest
Printing (Guangzhou, China), Co. Ltd; Job / Batch #:105283

For information address Wisdom Tales,
P.O. Box 2682, Bloomington, Indiana 47402-2682

www.wisdomtalespress.com

Everyone Prays

Celebrating Faith Around the World

By
Alexis York Lumbard

Illustrated by
Alireza Sadeghian

✤Wisdom Tales✤

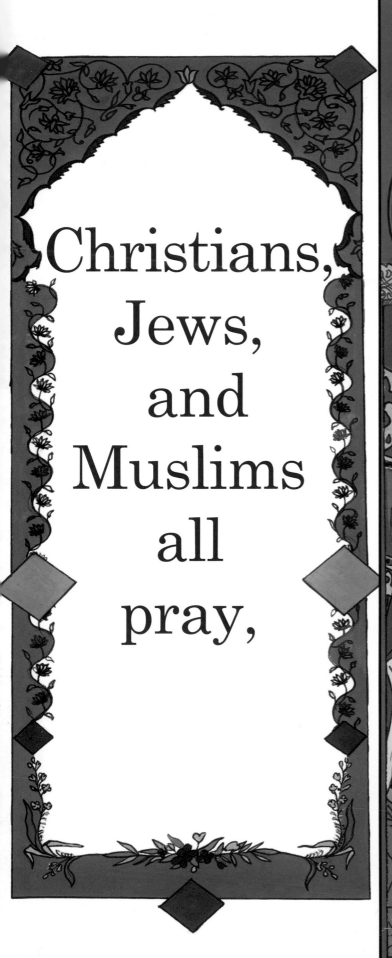

Christians,
Jews,
and
Muslims
all
pray,

and so do Hindus

3

and Buddhists.

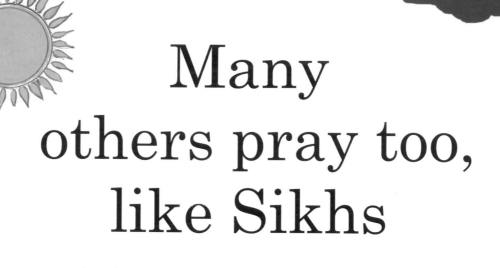

Many
others pray too,
like Sikhs

5

and Jains,

and those who
follow the
Shinto way.

People pray in different places like temples,

9

churches, or mosques,

while others
pray outside.

People pray with
different objects
like books,

13

beads, or candles.

14

Some pray

singing
and
dancing.

Others pray while quiet and still.

Some use water to clean themselves before they pray,

while others use it for special ceremonies.

Some pray with their heads covered,

19

but others do not.

People pray
when they are
happy, giving
thanks.

And people
pray when they
are sad, seeking peace.

Although people all over the world pray in different ways, it is to each heart the most precious light. So,

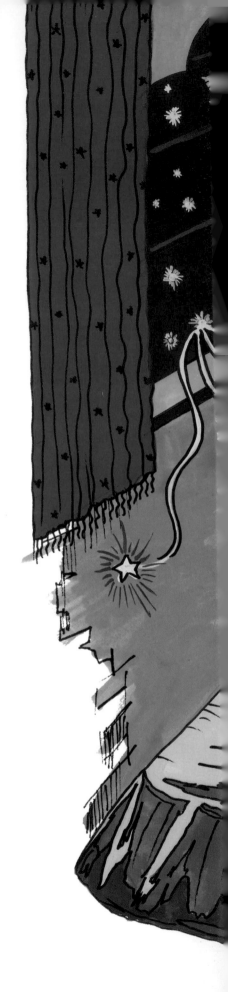

EVERYONE

PRAYS!

About the World's Religions

Have you ever wondered what the words *Jew*, *Christian*, *Muslim*, or *Buddhist* mean? These examples and many others refer to people who practice the religions of Judaism, Christianity, Islam, and Buddhism. The oldest meaning of the word *religion* is to "tie" or "bind." In other words, religion is how people the world over tie themselves to that which they hold sacred, like God or Heaven. One of the most important ways people of faith tie themselves to their beliefs is of course through prayer! Other ties include following the teachings of a founder or a holy book. Here are some helpful explanations:

 A *Jew* is someone who follows Judaism, a 3,500 year-old religion[1] based on the *Torah* revealed to the prophet Moses on Mount Sinai. The holy book of the Jews is the *Tanakh*, which is made up of the *Torah* and other books of the Jewish prophets. A Jewish place of prayer is called a synagogue.

 A *Christian* is someone who follows Christianity, a 2,000-year-old religion founded by Jesus Christ. The sacred book of Christianity is called the Bible. It includes both the New Testament as well as the Old Testament. Christians pray together in churches, monasteries, or meeting halls.

 A *Muslim* is someone who follows Islam, a 1,400-year-old religion based on the revelations sent to the prophet Muhammad in Arabia. The holy book of Islam is called the *Quran* and a Muslim house of prayer is called a mosque. Muslims pray to the same God as Christians and Jews, but they use the Arabic word for God, which is *Allah*.

Judaism, Christianity, and Islam all began in the part of the world known as the Middle East. Today Christianity (about 2 billion followers)[2] and Islam (about 1.5 billion) are the world's two largest religions, while Judaism has about 15 million followers.

 A *Hindu* is someone who follows Hinduism, a more than 4,000-year-old religion revealed to the ancient *rishis* or seers of India. Many of the holy scriptures of Hinduism are considered to be the *Vedas* and a Hindu place of worship is called a temple.

 A *Buddhist* is someone who follows Buddhism, a 2,500-year-old religion founded by the Buddha, Siddhartha Gautama. Buddhism's teachings are found in a collection of books called the *Sutras* and Buddhists gather to pray and meditate in temples and monasteries.

 A *Sikh* is someone who follows Sikhism, a 500-year-old religion founded by Guru Nanak. The holy book of Sikhism is called the *Guru Granth Sahib*, while Sikhs pray together in temples known as *gurdwaras*.

 A *Jain* is someone who follows Jainism, one of the oldest religions in the world. It has twenty-four founding teachers called *tirthankaras* and the last teacher, Mahavira, propagated the principle of non-violence in the 6th-5th centuries BCE. The Jain sacred books are called *agamas* and Jains come together to worship and meditate in Jain temples.

 A *Shintoist* is someone who follows Shintoism, the ancient religion of Japan called "the way of the gods." It does not have a founder or a sacred book but instead focuses on the holiness of the natural world. Shintoists pray at shrines in the home or in a special place in nature.

Hinduism (about 1 billion), Buddhism (about 500 million), Sikhism (about 30 million), and Jainism (about 5 million) all began in India, while Shintoism (about 50 million) has its origins in Japan.

Did you know that there are still many more religions in the world, such as the American Indian religions of North and South America, as well as the many traditional religions found in Africa? For more information please visit www.wisdomtalespress.com.

---

[1] As it is difficult to fix precise dates to the origin of many of the world's religions, the ages given are approximate.

[2] The figures listed are rough estimates of the number of adherents for each religion.

Illustration Notes

Everyone Prays takes us on a tour around the world. In this book we visit:

1-2: The inside of a church, synagogue, and mosque. The three Abrahamic religions of Judaism, Christianity, and Islam share a common belief in one God and have a common ancestor in the patriarch Abraham.

3-4: A pilgrimage to the Ganges River in India. Considered as sacred by both Hindus and Buddhists, pilgrims bathe in the river to purify themselves and seek spiritual blessings.

5: The Golden Temple of India, the most important house of worship for Sikhs. It was built by Guru Arjan, who also compiled the *Adi Granth*, the holy book of the Sikhs.

6: The statue of Gomateshvara Bahubali, also in India. This statue is one of the important pilgrimage destinations in Jainism.

7-8: A group of Shinto pilgrims proceed to the Itsukushima Shrine along the coast of Japan. The shrine is marked by a *tori* gate, a symbol which indicates the beginning of a sacred space, where Shintoists pay their respects to the gods or their ancestors.

9-10: The ancient city of Jerusalem which houses the Western Wall, the Church of the Holy Sepulcher, and the Dome of the Rock, among the holiest sites for Jews, Christians, and Muslims.

11-12: A coming of age dance for Maasai warriors of East Africa. The Maasai are a semi-nomadic people who believe in one God called Ngai. Their sacred dance often includes leaping up and down as a symbol of bravery and strength. Sacred song and dance are central to many African cultures.

13: A *Quran* school where boys and girls learn how to read the Muslim scripture, which is written and recited in Arabic.

14: An icon of Our Lady of Guadalupe, an image of the Virgin Mary venerated by Roman Catholics.

15: The Sun Dance ceremony of the North American Indians. It is one of the most important religious rites for the Plains Indians, intended for the spiritual renewal of its members and for the whole earth.

16: A North American Plains Indian on a vision quest, which involves the solitary practice of intensive prayer and fasting in order to seek out the Divine aid.

17: A courtyard of an Iranian mosque. Boys and men are performing *wudu*, which is the act of washing that Muslims must do before their five daily prayers.

18: Christian baptism in the river Jordan. In this sacred rite, Christians are cleansed of their sins, commit themselves to Jesus Christ, and formally enter the Christian faith.

19: A women's section of a mosque in Pakistan. Muslim women always cover their hair when they pray, while Muslim men often wear a small hat or turban. Both are signs of humility towards God.

20: A Buddhist temple in Myanmar. Buddhist monks and nuns all shave their heads as a sign of poverty and commitment to a holy life.

21: A Jewish American naming ceremony. Shortly after a baby is born, special prayers are said and the name of the child is publically given.

22: People of all faiths, in times of sadness or need, turn to Heaven for help and comfort.

23-24: People of many faiths say a special bedtime prayer, just like this Christian brother and sister. The following prayer is often used in Christian households: "Now I lay me down to sleep, I pray the Lord my soul to keep. If I shall die before I wake, I pray the Lord my soul to take. Amen."

25-26: Children praying from around the world. In many religions, the rainbow is a symbol of harmony between Heaven and earth.

"It's a Wide World of Faith"